Little House of Imaginary Distinctions

Little House of Imaginary Distinctions

Steven Carter

Hamilton Books
A member of
The Rowman & Littlefield Publishing Group
Lanham · Boulder · New York · Toronto · Plymouth, UK

Copyright © 2011 by
Hamilton Books
4501 Forbes Boulevard
Suite 200
Lanham, Maryland 20706
Hamilton Books Acquisitions Department (301) 459-3366

Estover Road
Plymouth PL6 7PY
United Kingdom

All rights reserved

British Library Cataloging in Publication Information Available

Library of Congress Control Number: 2011929165
ISBN: 978-0-7618-5600-9 (paperback : alk. paper)
eISBN: 978-0-7618-5601-6

In loving memory
of Cecil and Bessie Coleman,
maternal grandparents who provided an
angry adolescent comfort and shelter
at 2111 Grant Street in Berkeley—

Acknowledgments

As always, I wish to thank formatting editor Dorothy Albritton. Thanks also to assistant acquisitions editor Lindsay MacDonald of Rowman & Littlefield publishers.

Special thanks to Janice Carter for clarifying certain family anecdotes, especially ones concerning her unique and redoubtable dad.

Introduction

Look around you. The world is more homogeneous than you think. Far too often, distinctions among people, places, and things are matters of degree rather than kind. Many are illusory.

According to the big political picture, in America 2010—thanks to both the Democrats and the Republicans—we're all flailing about with one oar in the same leaky rowboat; but even bigger pictures (contrasting America with China, for example) prove deceptive. By now every man in the street knows, or ought to know, that political, social, and economic differences between the two great powers of East and West become more negligible by the day, so much so that I chose to define "China" in my *New Devil's Dictionary* as "A capitalist nation engaged in fierce economic rivalry with the People's Republic of the United States."

I tacked on a news item from the Associated Press:

> The Communist government of China presented its model worker award (in the past given to loyal factory workers, dedicated public-outhouse stewards and the like) to Yao Ming, the Houston Rockets basketball player who earns about $15,000,000 a year playing and endorsing products—about 15,000 times what the average Chinese worker makes.

Here's another example of "imaginary distinctions," this one from the other side of the world from Beijing and Shanghai—Paris.

Since Mark Twain and Henry James, millions of Americans have traveled to Europe primarily to discover America and their fellow Americans. Like James's Lambert Strether in *The Ambassadors and* Christopher Newman in *The American,* foreign faces and foreign places often make natives from Chagrin Falls, Ohio, and Spearfish, South Dakota, uneasy. (Las Vegas entrepreneurs understood this and eliminated the middleman by transplanting the Eiffel Tower, the Roman Circus and the Giza pyramid to Sin City).

I myself enjoy running into Americans in the cafes, bistros, and lobbies of the cheap, tall hotels in Paris; but I always draw the line at food. Not so two young American couples, friends of my son, who spent two-and-a-half weeks in Paris a number of years ago. They saw the sights and went to the museums, enduring the rude remarks and glances of Parisians who've been known to spit on Americans. (Of course one always resents one's benefactors. America's sin was to bail France out of two world wars.)

They had to eat, and here the distinction between things American and things Gallic dissolved into a lifeless mass. In the seventeen days and nights they spent in Paris, the two couples had no less than 50 meals—breakfast, lunch, and dinner—every single one at a handful of the seventy-three McDonalds scattered across Paris.[1]

—"The bower," Swan Lake, Montana

---

1. Money wasn't the issue. Paris teems with working-class restaurants, especially in Montparnasse, where you can get an excel-

---

lent meal for six dollars or less. The wonderful Restaurant des Milles Colonnes off the Rue Delambre is one such. In 1971 my wife and I enjoyed French cuisine, bread, and all the very drinkable vin ordinaire you could swill down for a buck a head. No one ever left that establishment broke or hungry.

Author's Note to the Reader

Little House of Imaginary Distinctions is meant to complement my previous volume *Little House of Oxymorons,* published by Hamilton Books in 2010.

Little House of Imaginary Distinctions

FOX News, 12/28/10:

"New York City public school teacher spends thirteen years in 'rubber room' with full pay."

Dollars to doughnuts he thought he was still in the classroom.

❧

1. Unfathomable stupidity. 2. Celebration injuries in football.

❧

"I'm *not* nagging, I'm just reminding you"—the eternal mantra.

❧

Years ago, a friend told me with a straight face, "It's not my feet that smell; it's my shoes."

ര്ക

. . . Sometimes lines between distinctions and similarities are deliberately ambiguous, as in Winston Churchill's famous assessment of Americans and Brits as "two peoples separated by a common language."

ര്ക

A mother's eternal excuse for the classroom washout: "Johnny is very intelligent, and has a real desire to learn, but he's bored by school."

When my wife was teaching second grade, a mother complained that her daughter, Eddy Lynn, was bored. At a conference—both mother and daughter were present—the mother reiterated her complaint. Eddy Lynn looked on with a smirk.

"Well," my wife said, "why don't I give Eddy Lynn some extra work to do so she won't be bored?"

The smirk—and the color—disappeared from Eddy Lynn's face. The mother was silent.

"I think we've found the source of Eddy Lynn's problem," my wife said.

ര്ക

Local weather guy in Bakersfield, CA: "Tomorrow's weather in the north valley will be clear but cloudy."

❧

Edith, my late grandmother-in-law's best friend, buried three husbands before throwing in the towel on marriage. She was quite a character. The world's worst driver, her motto was, "If you worry about the front end, the back end will take care of itself."

Like my grandmother-in-law, Edith had an epic addiction to chocolate. 100 pounds overweight, she also loved pastries, fried foods, pizza—the whole nine yards.

"But," she reassured her doctor, raising a forefinger, "I draw the line at bread."[1]

❧

Don't let anyone (especially Ernest Hemingway) tell you that putting the painful things in your life down on paper exorcises the demons. The demons stay right where they are; they just get written about.

❧

---

1. When ordered to drive to the hospital ASAP because of dangerously high blood pressure, Edith stopped off on the way for a chocolate malt or two.

Years ago, I came in on the tail end of a conversation about a certain vegetable.

". . . It's a very phallic-looking object."

Within earshot was Cindy, the precocious thirteen-year-old daughter of a family friend.

"I don't know about that," she interjected, "but I know what it looks like."

❧

A few months back, the girlfriend of a well-known Hollywood actor told a reporter,

"What I love about him is that he's a real pseudo-intellectual!"

As opposed to a phony pseudo-intellectual?

On another occasion, the same girl was quoted,

"I'm an atheist, but I do believe in a higher power."

❧

TV news descriptions of the recent Haitian earthquake varied from "temblor" to "tremor" to "trembler." Pick a word, any word.

❧

Wendy's slogan: "It's waaay better than fast food."

❧

An announcement on FOX sports:

"Due to contractual obligations we must leave this broadcast in a few minutes, but we hope you're enjoying the game."

This Division I NCAA football match was up for grabs, tied 28-28 in the fourth quarter, with a national ranking on the line.

❧

I love Diet Pepsi's slogan: "Zero calories, maximum taste."

❧

From an eighth-grade composition: "If your land is hilly, farm around it."

❧

Remember the famous 50's TV ad: "I'm not a doctor, but I play one on television"? (My postmodern spin: "I'm a doctor, but I don't play one on television.")

ക്ക

Miller Lite ad featuring "competing" has-been athletes and coaches: "Tastes great!" "Less filling!" "Tastes great!" "Less filling!"

. . . Much is made of the distinction between Bud Light and Miller Lite when, of course, like most mainstream American beers they both taste essentially the same—on a par with carbonated dishwater.

ക്ക

In a recent blind taste-test, a Gallo Chardonnay beat out a host of far more expensive wines, including imports.

ക്ക

On a number of occasions, I've witnessed the phenomenon of a spouse getting a divorce and "marrying the same person" all over again—sometimes more than once; same personality, same foibles, even the same looks.

Plus ca change, plus ca meme chose.

❧

When it comes to entertainment, Americans have a genius for buying the same used car two, three, four, even five or more times. I'm referring of course to movies and their sequels—*Death Wish; Rambo;* the Clint Eastwood spaghetti westerns and the *Dirty Harry* series; *Nightmare on Elm Street; Halloween* (now in its ninth incarnation); *Friday the Thirteenth,* etc. The template for these box office scams may have been *Rio Bravo,* made way back in '59, and its re-make, *El Dorado* from 1967. Like their descendants, these westerns were essentially clones of each other, down to the character played by Ricky Nelson, called Colorado in *Rio Bravo* and Mississippi in *El Dorado.*

And of course John Wayne always played John Wayne, Jack Nicholson always plays Jack Nicholson, Kevin Costner always plays Kevin Costner. . . .

❧

In the 1964 film version of the play *Becket*, Becket (Richard Burton) tells Henry II (Peter O'Toole), "Tonight at dinner I'm going to unveil a new invention—the fork. It's for spearing meat, so that your hands won't get dirty."

Henry mulls this over.

"But then you dirty the fork. I don't see the point."

❧

In the seventies, my redoubtable rancher father-in-law goes to Woolco, a proto-Wal-Mart. When he writes a check, the clerk says,

"Oh, sir—you made this out to K-Mart!"

"So I did," my father-in-law says, writing another check. "Well, hell," he adds, "it's the same crap, isn't it?

❧

As far as my father-in-law is concerned, all restaurants are the same, no matter what's on the menu. Reason: he always orders the wrong thing. The latest in a litany of "wrong dinners" was shark, which he foolishly ordered at an Italian restaurant. It came in the form of an oscillating cube, like a hunk of Jell-O.

After he finished, I asked him how he liked it.

"Well," he said, "it kind of left a question mark in my mind."

❧

When I was in my twenties, I was a passionate liberal. Now that I'm in my sixties, I'm a passionate conservative. Nothing has changed.

❧

The George W. Bush administration, under the tutelage of Dick Cheney and Karl Rove, refused to call water-boarding torture, preferring the pallid euphemism "enhanced interrogation techniques."

Try selling that to someone who's been water-boarded.

❧

In the wonderful film *Radio Days,* Woody Allen's parents are constantly bickering—if a bone of contention doesn't exist, they'll dig one up. At one point the father shouts, "Are you saying the Pacific is a greater ocean than the Atlantic?"

❧

Botanists talk all day about significant distinctions among poison oak, poison sumac, and poison ivy. Tell it to anyone who's had a close encounter with one, two, or all three.

❧

Forget all that blather about who was the better baseball player, Ruth or Cobb. Each played on an elevated level of excellence which makes contrasts odious.

Since you didn't ask, my vote for the greatest player of all time goes to the incomparable Willie Mays. He could hit (career BA of .302), hit for power (636 home runs), and run the bases like a jackrabbit. He was also the greatest defensive centerfielder in the history of the game.

Sometimes real distinctions are disguised as "same old, same old." Lots of people think the space program was and is a waste of time and money—the space shuttle, for example, going round and round in circles for three decades and getting nowhere.

Ask these folks how they'll feel when China and Russia set up shop on Mars and start selling us timeshares.

Check out these snippets from a recent syndicated newspaper article:

> "Oppositional Defiant Disorder (ODD) features the same behaviors expected during certain stages of a child's development."

So what's the difference between what's labeled ODD and what used to be called "acting like a spoiled brat"?

> "There's no clear cause, but ODD is likely to be a combination of inherited and environmental factors."

Right; so is everything else. Anyway, ODD joins a laundry list of fashionable "disorders," all of which have one thing in common: they allow the "sufferer" to evade responsibility for his or her behavior. (See below)

❧

My late mother-in-law on the subject of her mother:
"She's not nosey; she's interested."

❧

In the film A *River Runs through it,* younger son Paul changes the spelling of his last name from MacLean to McLean. The father is very upset.

". . . Now people will think we're Lowland Scots," he complains.

❧

Twin cities Midland and Odessa, Texas, look down on each other as being totally different—upscale Midland is considered snobbish by citizens of Odessa, who in turn are pooh-poohed as redneck and blue collar by folks in Midland. Insofar as both places are located in West Texas, one of the worst geographical areas on planet Earth, these distinctions are meaningless. West Texas is the setting for the film *No Country for Old Men.* Trust someone who's been there: no country for anyone else, either.

Ananke: Greek word for human destiny. What does that mean when the destiny of most of us is to have no destiny at all?

Thousands of lives were lost in Vietnam while the peace talks of 1971-74 stalled because the two sides couldn't agree on the shape of the bargaining table.

A student of mine at the University of Hawaii had been recently honorably discharged from the army. He informed me that he was still carrying shrapnel from an AK-47 round in his stomach. He was wounded in Laos "where," he said, "we weren't supposed to be in '66." Right, I was tempted to gently add—as opposed to Vietnam, where we belonged?

Hawaii vs. the politically correct Hawai'i? The ghost of King Kamehameha couldn't care less, but at least liberals at the U. of Hawaii can feel good about themselves.

Remember Ronald Reagan's anti-environmentalist remark from 1982, "If you've seen one redwood tree, you've seen them all"?

George, my curmudgeonly 85-year-old neighbor at Swan Lake, is hard of hearing. "I attended a city council meeting in Bigfork," he informed me the other day. When I asked him how it went, he replied, "Not too good; I only understood half of what they said—their voices are too damned soft!"

❧

Question: What's the difference between a French bourgeois and a German bourgeois? Answer: the French language and the German language.

That's a bit glib. French bourgeois are insufferable, but the Germans. . . . When introduced, they act as though meeting you was the low point of their week.

❧

Son Michael, who received his doctorate in sociology at UC Riverside earlier this year, is throwing his hat in the ring for what few jobs there are. One part-time teaching position at a California college features a ridiculously low salary, even for an adjunct gig. The ad concludes, however: "We realize the salary is low, but we treat our adjuncts with dignity and respect."

❧

In written and spoken discourse, isn't replacing "he" with "she" merely substituting one brand of bullshit with another? Jonathan Swift and Mark Twain would've been all over this and other excesses of political correctness like a cheap suit.

❧

Luc, the four-year-old son of my wife's California friend Susan, was in a pre-school Christmas play. He said, "I'm not going to be a real lamb, Mom. I'll be wearing a costume."

❧

One of the dumbest imaginary distinctions I know of comes from—where else?—academia. Community college administrators have been addicted for years to the inane and insane mantra of "Goals and Objectives" in curricula. I taught in the community college for over ten years, and no one ever provided me with any meaningful distinction between a goal and an objective. More silly and self-perpetuating in-house jargon. . . . Once again, Jonathan Swift would've pounced, especially in Part III of *Gulliver's Travels*.

❧

Recently an eighteen-year-old boy strangled his ten-year-old brother. In his own defense, he told authorities, "I felt like I was on the ceiling, looking down at me doing it."

Bingo! Not guilty of murder by reason of "Dissociative Disorder."

⁂

In the outcome of a civil suit how many times have you heard of a corporation agreeing to pay all fines, damages, costs, etc., while "admitting no guilt?" Excuse me?

⁂

No difference at all between Paradise and Palo Alto, Calif., for a young boy growing up on the south Peninsula, as I did in the fifties. That was when Silicon Valley was just the Santa Clara Valley, and apple, cherry, and peach orchards still dominated the landscape. No longer: by the eighties[2] not a single orchard remained.

⁂

---

2. Before I was born, San Franciscans hopped on south-bound "blossom-viewing" trains that slowly wound through the orchards, stopping here and there so the passengers could get off, enjoy leisurely picnics under the flowering trees, and head back home when the trains made the return trip.

Yesterday the addled President of Iran told the U.N. General Assembly, "We do take United Nations sanctions seriously, which is not the same thing as believing they are effective."

❧

Flotsam and jetsam.

❧

Because Rosencrantz and Guildenstern share the same lack of conscience, they have no individuality—no souls. Shakespeare underscores their interchangeability by having Claudius and Gertrude greet them, "Welcome, good Rosencrantz and gentle Guildenstern"; and "Welcome, good Guildenstern and gentle Rosencrantz."

❧

Alphonse and Gaston are famous characters in French farce—clones, insofar as each constantly tells the other, "No, sir, after you," "No, sir, after *you*," etc. In baseball, the Alphonse and Gaston play is so named because occasionally outfielders circling under a fly ball will look at each other—"I got it," "no, I got it,"—until the ball drops between them for a hit.[3]

❧

In restaurants in the state of Utah, you can't order a double gin and tonic; you can order two single g and t's. Go figure.

❧

In another Woody Allen film—I forget which one—the Woody Allen character asks a young rock music aficionado—real airhead, addicted to the neologism "trans-splendid"—if she's a groupie.

"No," she shakes her head, "but I do like to follow bands on the road."

"Interesting distinction."

❧

---

3. Also known as the husband and wife play—no communication.

Humans and chimps share 99% of the same genes. Some would say that's a tad conservative.

❧

—Oh, God, another in an infinite, and I do mean infinite, series of TV cop dramas, *Detroit 1-8-7* "stands apart from all the rest!" Uh-huh. "Different city, different actors, same crap," as my father-in-law would say.

❧

A modern Irish poet once said, "It's a terrible, terrible thing not having gainful employment." Then he added, "The only worse thing would be actually having a job."

❧

When a madman hears voices in his head, they lock him up. When a writer hears voices in his head, they give him a prize.

❧

Barstow, Calif., vs. hell? The issue is finely balanced.

❧

Gila Bend, Az., vs. hell? Ditto.

❧

Teens, bless their hearts, have always been addicted to imaginary distinctions. When I was in junior high and high school, Levis were cool, Wranglers and Billy the Kid jeans most definitely un-cool. For guys cruising the drag, the most important thing in the world was the shotgun—front passenger—seat, never mind that the dude riding in back was traveling at the same speed and arrived at the same destination at the same time.

❧

The S.F. Giants and the Chicago Cubs—different towns, different fan bases, different ballparks: one rich in ivy-covered tradition, the other postmodern . . . and yet, and yet; when it comes to disappointing their fans year after year, decade after decade—in the Cubs' case century after century—these two impoverished nations of baseball's third world are near-clones. My poor Giants won their last World Championship in 1954, when they swept the heavily-favored Cleveland Indians. The Cubs—who captured their last World Series during the Third Punic War (actually 1908)—haven't been to a fall classic since 1945.

. . . All this in spite of a roster of superstars gracing both ball clubs over the decades—Ron Santo, Ferguson Jenkins, Greg Maddox, Mark Grace, Billy Williams, and the great Ernie Banks for the Cubbies, and Willie McCovey, Juan Marichal, Orlando Cepeda, Jack Sanford, and, of course Willie Mays for the Giants.

As we speak, the Giants enjoy a one-game lead in the National League West over the San Diego Padres, with seven games to go in the regular season. Could this be the year? With the Yankees hiding in the tall weeds over in the American League, probably not.[4]

❧

. . . And how about the imaginary distinction between tap water and bottled water "from fresh mountain streams"? Actually, there *is* a distinction—if you don't mind traces of beaver scat in your bottled water.

❧

---

4. Like most of my sports predictions, happily this one went south, big time. The Giants plowed through the Braves and the Phillies to reach the World Series, where they clobbered the Texas Rangers four games to one! This brings to mind Shelley's immortal rhetorical question: "If the Giants win it all, can the Cubs be far behind?"

By now we're all accustomed to the greater variety of "news" we're bombarded with 24/7, the more uniformly trivial and meaningless it is. This morning on CNN Headline News: *World's largest shoe store opens in London; Robber injured diving into dumpster; Lady Gaga speaks out against "Don't ask, don't tell,"* etc. etc.

ꕥ

Left brain, right brain—yes, the distinctions between these two seats of human intelligence are profound, but what does that matter when people by the tens of millions get off on junk like "Dancing with the Stars" and "American Idol"?

ꕥ

Discussing stun-guns and tasers with a cop, a TV reporter uses the phrase "non-lethal." The cop interjects, "We prefer to say, "less than lethal."

ꕥ

Boones Farm and Strawberry Hill. . . . Uh-huh.

ꕥ

Question put to a FOX news panel: "So . . . comedian Stephen Colbert's appearance before Congress—funny or a farce?

How about Congress itself? Funny or a farce?

❧

Barbara Boxer vs. Carly Fiorina in the 2010 California Senate race? *That* was the only choice we had? Sweet fancy Moses. . . .

❧

Line from a poem published in a recent issue of *Big Muddy*:

". . . And the Tenderloin, swarming with whores and prostitutes. . . ."

❧

Celebrity endorser on TV: "Folks, I honestly believe in this product; I wouldn't use it if I didn't. But don't just take my word for it. . . ."

❧

How many photos of rock bands have you seen on TV, in newspapers and magazines during the last four decades—all looking the same: pretending to be angry, long-haired, defiant, rebellious, etc. Of course they laugh all the way to the bank, and—rock music being the most potent aphrodisiac on the planet—they get laid all they want. So what're they angry about?

Remember NFL broadcasters Pat Summerall and John Madden? —Both equally execrable, both suffering from that wasting disease of the frontal lobes known as logorrhea. . . .

The ACLU insists that they're not an organization biased toward liberalism, that they defend the rights of the Left and the Right with equal fervor. Don't believe a word of it. When's the last time you recall a conservative group or individual being represented by the ACLU?

Let me add to the mix "The City," by C.P. Cavafy, the greatest Greek poet of the 20th century:

> You said, "I'll go to another country, another shore,
> find another city better than this one.
> Whatever I try to do is fated to turn out wrong
> and my heart lies buried as though it were something dead.
> How long can I let my mind molder in this place?
> Wherever I turn, wherever I happen to look,
> I see the black ruins of my life, here,
> where I've spent so many years, wasted them,
> destroyed them utterly."
>
> You won't find another country, won't find another shore,
> this city will always pursue you. You will walk
> the same streets, grow old in the same neighborhoods,
> will turn gray in these same houses.
> You will always end up in this city.
> Don't hope for things elsewhere:
> there is no ship for you, there us no road,
> as you've wasted your life here, in this small corner,
> you've destroyed it everywhere else in the world.

❧

Arthur C. Clarke's Law: "Any sufficiently advanced form of technology is indistinguishable from magic."

❧

Billy Martin, Bob Lemon, Dick Howser, Joe Torre, Joe Girardi—different managing styles, different temperaments, different rosters of pitching and hitting coaches. What does that matter if the House of Steinbrenner routinely buys up every superstar in major league baseball?

The World Series? Bought and paid for.[5]

❧

I still love Monty Python's transition from one sketch to another, equally hysterical sketch: "And now for something completely different."

❧

The House of Capulet and the House of Montague. . . Shakespeare was the second great poet—after Homer in the *Iliad*— to document that such warring houses always share the same basement—hell.

❧

---

5. Not this year (2010). The Yankees were smoked in the ALCS by the Texas Rangers.

Hippies and beatniks—

Sociologists go through reams of printer paper parsing out distinctions between the two subcultures; bottom line is that they both constituted retreats from responsibility—from reality itself—where losers could have a day in the sun.

Church camp and Gomorrah—

Certainly the pastor will insist on a world of differences. Not in my experience, thank Eros.

Bottom-screen news blurb on FOX news yesterday:

BIZZARE DEATH

. . . Yes, but FOX's (and CNN's) misspellings these days are legion. Keep in mind that apostrophe goofs are classified by usage experts as spelling errors.

First and second opinions—

What's the difference if they're both wrong? This has happened more than once in my experience.

❧

Who and *whom*—forget it.

❧

Healthy and *healthful*—forget it.

❧

The critic Quentin Crisp tells a wonderful anecdote about a question-and-answer session following one of his lectures in Britain. In response to a query about his religious persuasion, he announced that he was an atheist, whereupon a woman rose. "Yes," she acknowledged, "but is it the God of the Protestants or the God of the Catholics in whom you don't believe?"

❧

"Paper or plastic?"

"*You* decide."

❧

Kim Jong Il (president of North Korea) and Mahmoud Ahmadinejad (president of Iran). Enough said.

❧

Jimmy Carter and Warren G. Harding. Dead heat.[6]

❧

Three films have been made of Fitzgerald's *The Great Gatsby*: 1929, 1949, and 1973. All three suck. Almost without exception, you can't turn a great novel into a great movie.

❧

---

6. Carter's Nobel Peace Prize, like Al Gore's and especially Barack Obama's, was a joke. Carter had almost nothing personally to do with the peace pact between Israel and Egypt, except to panic when Anwar Sadat threatened to bail on the proceedings in Washington. Seeing the Nobel slipping out of his grasp, Carter did everything but fall on his knees and beg so that Sadat would stick around and complete the process.

Napoleon said, "England is a nation of shopkeepers." So was France. So why were they at war? The Little General couldn't answer that one.

☙

Junk bonds (2001) and French war bonds (1915)—to your Aunt Sophie and her great-great aunt Sophie, same old, same old.

☙

Stanford and Harvard—in our time of universal political correctness in academia, same far-Left humanities curricula, same radicalized undergrads (especially English majors); same disregard for the civil rights of conservative opponents (the Stanford student legislature attempted to prevent conservative dissidents from voting).

Stanford even calls itself the Harvard of the West—which brings one more common link to mind: snobbishness.

☙

School boards and idiots. . . . Mark Twain: "First, God made idiots. That was for practice. Then he made school boards."

This school year the Helena, MT, school board voted to install sex education curricula in the lower grades—nothing new, except that fifth-graders were to be taught different sexual positions, and second-graders were to be taught about homosexuality. Naturally the parents revolted.

❧

As of late summer of 2010, House Speaker Nancy Pelosi and British Petroleum are equally unpopular with the American public. Given BP's wretched excesses in the Gulf of Mexico, that's quite an achievement—even for the smug, insufferable Pelosi.

❧

Let's see—Clint Eastwood, Kevin Costner, Nicholas Cage, Tom Cruise, Keanu Reeves, Russell Crowe. . . . Undo the polymath, please.

❧

After 38 years of correcting students' apostrophe errors—it's for its and its for it's—inevitably I started doing it myself. No teacher left behind.

❧

Joe Lieberman's voice and a pan of water on low boil. . . . Ah, but you gotta love Joe.

❧

Don't you love it when politicians—all politicians—insist at one time or other, "I'm not a politician." Such is the pejorative state that word has sunk to.

❧

Yesterday, *n.* Tomorrow.

❧

Pit bulls and their masters—here, too, the issue is finely balanced.

ꕥ

Erwin Rommel and George S. Patton—mortal enemies; still, they were peas in a pod insofar as both admired each other; both were brilliant, daring, and innovative field commanders; both were contemptuous of Brit Field Marshall Bernard Law Montgomery; both loved horses (Patton liked to refer to himself as an "old horse cavalryman"); both fell out of favor with their senior commanders (Rommel was obliged to commit suicide). If circumstances permitted, I know they would've enjoyed sitting down and splitting a bottle of French cognac—which they both liked.

ꕥ

When my wife Janice and her friend Susan volunteered to do puppet shows in the Tucson public schools, they were required—of course—to fill out a plethora of forms in triplicate. According to an assistant principal, they were required to use pencil—not ink.

"The form will be voided if you use ink," he explained.

The forms read: *Make sure there are no erasures or crossings-out or this document will be voided.* So why not ink?

ꕥ

In his wonderful taxonomies of love, the French novelist Stendhal discusses passion-love, but never addresses the issue of what I call *panic-love,* an entity composed of two emotions which, at the apex of a love affair, become virtually indistinguishable.

When two lovers are "in the throes" of passion, they can't get enough of each other. Even sex can't or won't mitigate the desire for more—more sex, but also more closeness, affection, and, of course, the silliness of "What are you thinking?" "No, what are *you* thinking?" etc. As we know, like Camelot, the brief kingdom of this desire doesn't endure; but while it lasts it becomes—may become—downright scary: What if I can never get enough of this person—forever? What if, *au fond*, there's a symbiotic relationship between love and frustration; what if love *is* frustration 24/7?

Now that I'm in my late sixties this seems like nonsense; and yet it is, or was, real. When younger I felt the hot whips of panic-love in connection with two or three individuals. And, in the process of being scourged, the feeling swept over me that *this* is what Mr. Congreve called the way of the world: nothing less than an infernal conspiracy against human happiness.

❧

Ark and *Arc*: two different words, two different meanings. So why do more than twelve million Americans believe that Joan of Arc was Noah's wife?

❧

UFOs, ESP, ghosts, poltergeists, teleportation, telekinesis, Nostradamus,[7] angels singing hymns at the Pearly Gates—all the rest of that business.

P.S.: Don't forget astrology—especially astrology.

❧

Twitter and Facebook—the latter slightly more popular than the former as we speak, but in truth they're equal co-conspirators in this wretched and retrograde era of information-overkill.

❧

When our son was nearly two, my wife was bathing him one afternoon when she noticed two small turds on the edge of the bathtub.

"Michael, what's this?"

"This one's a dot and that one's a turtle."

❧

---

7. Among his predictions: There will be a great war in the twentieth century. Uh-huh; and the seventeenth, and the eighteenth, and the nineteenth; not to mention the twenty-first and beyond.

Talk all you want about biodiversity, but in the end what's the un-avowed purpose of virtually all flora and fauna in the country around our desert home in AZ? To mess up your world.

❧

McCarthyism and political correctness—little fundamental difference, even though one entity was on the Right and the other is on the Left. A demand for unthinking conformity is just one bottom line shared by these two forms of fascism.

❧

"After your call, please stay on the line for a brief survey about our services." A.k.a. a sales pitch.

❧

"*Prostate* gland?" says a local (northwest Montana) farmer incredulously to his doctor. "All this time I thought it was my phosphate gland giving me problems."

❧

In the 19th century, the following exchange took place between two U.S. Senators.

The first (rubbing his hand on the other's bald head): "Smooth as my wife's behind!"

The second: "Why, so it is."

❧

What do differences between British and American spelling matter when the words refer to the same thing? Who cares about "judgment" and "judgement" at the Final Picking?

❧

. . . Let's not forget the ever-popular TV chestnut, "Free gift." As opposed to a gift that comes with a price tag?

❧

Cf. the names of towns in predominantly lockstep-Mormon Utah—Standardville, Centerville, Circleville, Orderville, Blandingsville—for good measure I'll throw in Virgin.

Talk about "if you've seen one, you've seen 'em all"!

❧

Question: for today's "non-traditional" students, what's the difference between going back to college and a shopping trip to the mall? Answer: nothing, as long as their attitude toward education is as something "to get out of the way."

When I was still teaching, Heaven help the student who used that phrase in my presence. European students of all ages I've taught on both sides of The Pond would never think in such hollow, pragmatic terms. Only in America do a student and "another satisfied customer" become indistinguishable.

(This is particularly true, needless to say, of on-line diploma mills like the University of Phoenix, Brown Mackie College, and a dozen others.

Remember the rubber stamp "adult" Westerns of the fifties? Not "adult" by today's crass standards—even though movies classified as M for Mature are targeted at audiences with an ontological age of twelve.

At a dinner party back in the thirties, George Bernard Shaw asked the woman seated next to him,

"Madam, if I gave you a million pounds, would you have sexual intercourse with me?"

"Why, I believe I would."

"And if I gave you five pounds?"

"Sir, what kind of woman do you think I am?"

"I thought we had established that, and were merely haggling over the price."

❧

. . . And what about the scores of jobs you desperately applied for back in the seventies and eighties—different towns (Spearfish, South Dakota; Odessa, Texas; Waukesha, Wisconsin), different schools, different teaching loads, all knit together by profound gratitude that you didn't get them?

❧

L.A. and San Francisco—apples and oranges, yes, save for one thing—narcissism.

❧

Hitler and Napoleon—a smorgasbord of differences, but one common thread—their insane decisions to invade Russia in winter. Hitler had Napoleon's mistake to learn from, but. . . .[8]

ঌ৵

An AA degree? In most cases that and ten bucks will get you a double latte at Starbucks.

ঌ৵

Oprah and Ellen—fundamentally the same, except for 1) sexual orientation and 2) the fact that Ellen doesn't think she's Mother Teresa.

ঌ৵

---

8. This was just one of a litany of critical blunders made by Hitler: bombing London, a non-military target, while letting the RAF off the hook; waiting three days before finishing off the British troops at Dunkirk, allowing them to escape by sea; ignoring his generals' pleas to bring two Panzer divisions from Calais to Normandy once the invasion was on (Hitler insisted Operation Overlord, which featured the largest naval armada in human history, was a decoy); refusing to re-supply Erwin Rommel with petrol in North Africa, giving Montgomery the upper hand; repeating Napoleon's error by invading Russia in the cold months—so many mistakes that some Freudian-minded commentators, including me, think that unconsciously Hitler lost World War II on purpose.

The twelve-person jury system and the New York Yankees' 27 World Series championships: Too damn many.

❧

The amateur Freudian Norman Mailer used to distinguish between good and bad orgasms. Woody Allen's response: "Never had a bad orgasm. Every one was right on the money."

❧

The other day a jogging acquaintance and I were talking about Russian history. Catherine the Great came up—Catherine, who enjoyed sexual intercourse with animals and who died when the leather sling suspending a horse over her bed snapped—plopping the beast onto her chest.

My acquaintance looked at me. "I thought it was a mule. Sure it was a horse?"

"Absolutely. Catherine was an empress. She had better taste than to have sex with mules."

❧

Good money, bad money—apples and apples if you happen to embrace the same kind of wacky investment schemes as poor Mark Twain over a century ago.

❧

College mascots—the Oregon Duck; the Georgetown bulldog (the school's nickname is "Hoya": go figure); my California Golden Bears' Oskie; and (especially) the idiotic Stanford tall tree. (Oskie and the tall tree got into a real fight once on the basketball court at Stanford's Maples Pavilion.)

Can you say, "Stupid across the board"?

ூ

How about the traditional Stanford Indians vs. the politically correct Stanford Cardinal? Same third- and fourth-tier football and basketball teams, etc.[9] Why make the change? So radicalized faculty and students can feel good about themselves ("Native Americans," a fraction of one percent of whom attend Stanford anyway, could care less).

P.S.: Why "Cardinal?"

ூ

For that matter, why is "Native Americans" preferable to "Indians?"

A parable:

In Heart Butte, Montana, on the Blackfoot Reservation, there's a small bar frequented almost exclusively by Indians.

---

9. To be fair, Stanford's football team won the 2011 BCS Orange Bowl.

One day a white liberal pops in and bellies up to the bar, where rows of hunting knives mark the places of patrons gone to the head.

"You're not an Indian," he says to the guy knocking down shots of Jim Beam next to him. "You're a Native American."

Fortunately, the liberal is already bald.

Pick a revolution, any revolution. What goes around comes around.

Memory loss—the great leveler. Friend of my wife at a reunion: "Did you major in art or was that me?"

MGM, Paramount, Columbia. One casting couch was as soft as another.

Nazi Germany's superiority complex—a mere manifestation of that Teutonic inferiority complex rooted in muddy, centuries-deep historical soil.

❧

Deconstruction and sophistry: twins at the same business.

❧

The EPA and teats on a bull: 1+1=1.

❧

FEMA and teats on a bull: 1+1=1.

❧

The Department of Education and teats on a bull: 1+1=1.

❧

"Consider the alternative." Maybe, but as Ambrose Bierce would've been the first to tell you, alternatives to the status quo are usually equally bad, if not worse.

From *Gulliver's Travels* [on the underlying cause of the war between Lilliput and Blefescu]:

> . . . Which two mighty powers have been engaged in a most obstinate War for six and thirty Moons past. It began upon the following Occasion. It is allowed on all Hands, that the primitive way of breaking Eggs before we eat them, was upon the larger end; but his present Majesty's grandfather, while he was a boy, going to eat an egg, and breaking it according to the ancient Practice, happened to cut one of his fingers. Whereupon the Emperor his father, published an Edict, commanding all his Subjects, upon great Penalties, to break the smaller end of their Eggs. The People so highly resented this Law, there have been six Rebellions raised on that Account; wherein one Emperor lost his life, and another his Crown. These Civil Commotions were constantly fomented by the Emperor of Blefescu; and when they were quelled, the Exiles always fled [from Lilliput] for refuge to that Empire. It is computed, that Eleven Thousand Persons have, at several Times, suffered Death, rather than submit to break their Eggs at the smaller End. . . .

To have instant replay or not to have instant replay?

"Better to get it right"—so say the proponents. Yes and no. After watching zillions of NFL and college games featuring instant replay, I've come to the following conclusions. In fully three-fourths, probably more, of instances where plays are "under further review," the call on the field is upheld, making five riveting minutes of watching referees watch video monitors a waste of time. Plus, in order for a play to be overturned, "conclusive evidence" must be obtained, meaning that the outcome of an end-zone catch is *still* ambiguous. This makes the black and white distinction between getting it right and getting it wrong a further waste of time.

In retrospect, almost always the small number of calls which *are* overturned have no bearing on the outcome of the game, making the infinitesimal number of actual pivotal situations negligible, at least when weighed against the (by now) hundreds of hours of down time watching the solemn foolery of replay reviews while coaches, players, and the other refs stand around staring into space.

One more thing: like kudzu, instant replay is creeping into every nook and cranny of professional and college football games. It's just a matter of time until penalties (especially pass interference) and fourth-down calls will be under review, slowing games to the pace of pouring molasses in winter. And if football is inundated with Instant Replay, can baseball be far behind? How about questionable fouls in basketball?

In my jaundiced opinion, for 50 years or more the NFL and NCAA got along just fine without IR.

Speaking of football. . . . Since 1970, a culture has grown up around NFL Monday Night Football (as if we didn't get enough on Thursdays and Sundays, not to mention Saturdays during the playoffs.) No matter who happens to be playing, Monday night is meant to be something special, standing apart from other games. As far as I can see, the only thing different about MNF is the obnoxious and overheated Hank Williams Jr., who screams "ARE YOU READY FOR SOME FOOTBALL?" over and over at the top of his lungs to kick off the show.

ಹ್ಞ

The other day John Boehner, House minority whip, told the press, "I don't believe in compromise. What I believe in is common ground."

ಹ್ಞ

America—the only country in the world where it's simultaneously a sin *and* a sacrament to be wealthy. Why do Washington Democrats, 90% of whom are extremely well off, continually propose and pass legislation demonstrating a collective hatred of the rich? Guilt trips—perhaps; hypocrisy—yes, of course: but there's more to it than that.

Precisely who do Democrats think they're referring to when they cast stones at "the rich?" Presumably anyone who deserves to be zapped by the estate tax, which has been as high as an unbelievable 55%;[10] and yet of all taxes, the death tax is the most fluid, waxing and waning like a bad moon while opposing administrations come and go. As recently as thirty years ago, maybe twenty, if you were a millionaire, most Americans considered you to be unusually wealthy; no longer; at present tens of millions of Americans are millionaires. The Democrats don't seem to get this, or, if they do, they still paint the truly wealthy and the merely well-to-do with the same broad brush.

Why is it a sin and a sacrament to be rich in this country? Why, in the eyes of Democrats and many other Americans, is the psychological distinction between the two dispensations imaginary?

The truth is that when it comes to riches, America is nothing if not schizophrenic. On the one hand we have the homespun American dream of getting rich, bequeathed to us by Ben Franklin and the Puritans who, contrary to popular belief, saw nothing wrong with earthly wealth. And yet so many of us also feel compelled to punish the rich. These polarized attitudes rest on two wobbly assumptions: the rich don't deserve what they have because they somehow acquired it in spite of the American virtues of hard work and sacrifice—qualities the middle class likes to attribute to itself alone. The illogic of this reverse snobbery is self-evident. The other assumption is that some, maybe most, of the rich inherited at least part of their money and therefore don't deserve it twice over.

---

10. Keep in mind that in many cases this is money already taxed many times over—income taxes, capital gain taxes, past inheritance taxes, etc.

Bottom line: very few middle-class Americans, not to mention the Democrats in Washington, subscribe to the Old Testament fate-bound strictures of "the sins of the fathers"—*until the rich come to mind.*

"The wealthy can afford to help America," Democrat Joe Lieberman pontificated before becoming an Independent. Lieberman missed the point. For the old conservative cliché still holds water: liberal Washingtonians really are less interested in the vague prospect of "helping America" than they are in taking from the rich and giving to the poor—even the middle class. As we speak (December 16, 2010), the beat goes on in the House, which is scheduled to vote on the President's tax package[11] this week. The debate is sure to be loud, rancorous—probably vicious; and yet few politicos on both sides of the aisle will fully grasp what the shouting is truly about.[12]

---

11. They'll vote on whether to extend the Bush-era tax cuts another two years. The measure will certainly pass; what remains to be seen is how much the Dems succeed in savaging the President's proposal.

12. This just in: the vote passed the House on December 18 and the President signed the bill into law the next day. Republicans were thrilled; Democrats, frustrated and humiliated, were particularly angry about a new ten million dollar exemption plugged into the estate tax. In an unusually rude expression of partisanship, even for the Hill, House Speaker Nancy Pelosi and Senate Majority Leader Harry Reid snubbed the ceremony.

The four year-old great-grandson of a family friend is "a very good boy, but he always finds himself in trouble." The other day he was told not to cross the road in front of the house. Sure enough, half an hour later there he was on the other side. "Didn't I tell you not to cross the road?" his mother scolded. "I didn't cross the road," he said. "I went through the culvert."

❧

My 94-year-old father-in-law now lives in a nursing home in Choteau, MT. A year or two ago, during a visit from my wife, he pushed his dinner plate away.

"This meat tastes like boiled owl," he said.

Amused, my wife asked,

"Have you ever eaten boiled owl?"

"No. And *this* "—he tapped the plate with a fingernail—"is indicative of why I never eat boiled owl."

❧

"I want to spend more time with my family," or: "I betrayed the trust of my constituents, got caught, and resigned."

❧

"Nigerian police were given shoot-to-kill orders to quell street violence in Lagos."

ത്ത

After President Obama called for more civility in public discourse, House Republicans agreed to change their description of Obamacare from "job-killing" to "job-crushing."

ത്ത

On an Atlantic voyage in 1867, Mark Twain describes a fellow passenger as an "unsmiling sanctimonious old iceberg that looked like he was waiting for a vacancy in the Trinity." Twain overheard this person actually ask the captain if he planned to stop the ship on Sundays.

ത്ത

Alfred Hitchcock was famously misquoted as saying, "Actors are cattle." Hitchcock countered, "I never said that. What I said was, 'Actors should be treated like cattle.'"

ത്ത

About the Author

In 2005 Steven Carter retired as Emeritus Professor of English after teaching in the university for thirty-eight years. The author of seventeen books published here and abroad, he served as Senior Fulbright Fellow at two Polish universities in 1991. He is the only two-time winner of UNESCO's coveted *Nuove Lettere* International Poetry and Literature Prize. In 2010 he was awarded the Eric Hoffer Foundation's Montaigne Medal grand prize for his book of essays, *Devotions to the Text.* Carter and his wife Janice divide the year between Arizona and Montana.